CONGREGATION FOR C

PONTIFICAL WORK FOF

Pastoral Guidelines for
Fostering Vocations
to Priestly Ministry

Libreria Editrice Vaticana

United States Conference of Catholic Bishops
Washington, DC

Contents

Introduction

1. The Plenary Assembly of the *Congregation for Catholic Education*[1] has requested the publication of pastoral guidelines for fostering vocations to priestly ministry.

In response to this request, the *Pontifical Work for Priestly Vocations*, in collaboration with its consultors, with representatives of the Congregations for the Evangelization of Peoples, for the Oriental Churches, for Institutes of Consecrated Life and Societies of Apostolic Life, and for the Clergy, prepared a *Questionnaire about the Pastoral Ministry for Priestly Vocations*, so as to have an up-to-date overview of vocational pastoral ministry in the different parts of the world, especially as regards the ministerial priesthood.

On 15 March 2008, the *Questionnaire* was sent, via the Apostolic Nunciatures, to all the delegates of the Bishops' Conferences for the pastoral ministry for vocations, as well as to the directors of the "National Vocational Offices," so that they could provide information on the situation of vocations and formulate suggestions for pastoral action.

The analysis of the replies to the *Questionnaire* from the Bishops' Conferences and the National Offices showed that there was a demand for guidelines for vocational pastoral ministry, based on a clear and well-founded theology of vocation and of the identity of the ministerial priesthood.

I

The Pastoral Care of Vocations to Priestly Ministry in Today's World

2. The situation of priestly vocations is very varied in the world today. It seems to be characterized by both good and bad. While in the West there is the problem of a decline in vocations, in other continents, despite their lack of resources, there is a promising increase in priestly vocations.

In traditionally Christian countries, the worrying fall in the number of priests, the rising of their average age and the requirements of the new evangelization are shaping a new situation for the Church.[2]

The reduced birthrate also contributes to the diminishing of vocations to a special consecration. The life of the Catholic faithful is suffering the effects of the unbridled quest for material goods and the fall in religious practice, which discourage making courageous and demanding Gospel choices.

Therefore, as the Holy Father Benedict XVI has written: "Precisely in our time we know very well how those who were invited first say "no." Indeed, Western Christianity, the new "first guests," now largely excuse themselves; they do not have time to come to the Lord."[3]

However much the pastoral ministry for vocations in Europe and in the Americas is organized and creative, the results obtained do not correspond to the efforts made. Nevertheless, along with the difficult situations, which one must look at with courage and truth, there are some signs of recovery, above all where clear and challenging proposals of Christian life are offered.

3. The Christian community's prayer has always reinforced in the people of God a shared awareness with regard to vocations, a sense of a "spiritual solidarity."[4] Wherever an integrated pastoral ministry—with families, young people or in the mission field—develops and grows together with a pastoral ministry for vocations, there is a flowering of priestly vocations. The local Church becomes truly "responsible for the birth and development of priestly vocations."[5] Thus, the vocational dimension is not simply the adding on of programs and suggestions, but becomes the natural expression of the whole community.

The statistical data of the Catholic Church and several pieces of sociological research highlight that, when new evangelization initiatives are promoted in parishes, associations, ecclesial communities, and movements,[6] young people show themselves to be open to God's call and to offering their lives in the service of the Church.

The *family* remains the primary community for the transmission of the Christian faith. It can be seen everywhere that many priestly vocations are born in families where the example of a Christian life in keeping with its calling and the practice of the evangelical virtues give rise to the desire for complete self-giving. Care for vocations presupposes, in reality, a strong family pastoral ministry.

It should be added that often the question of vocations to the priesthood is sparked in boys and young men as a result of the joyful witness of priests.

The witness of priests united to Christ, happy in their ministry and united in brotherhood among themselves, has a strong vocational appeal for young men. Bishops and priests offer to young men a high and attractive image of ordained priesthood. "The very life of priests, their unconditional dedication to God's flock, their witness of loving service to the Lord and to his Church—a witness marked by free acceptance of the cross in the spirit of hope and Easter joy— their fraternal unity and zeal for the evangelization of the world are the first and most convincing factor in the growth of vocations."[7]

In reality, priests are often witnesses to being dedicated to the Church, to the capacity for joyful generosity, to adapting humbly to the different situations where they find themselves working. Their example gives rise in others to the desire to undertake great commitment in the Church and the wish to give one's life to the Lord and one's brethren.[8] In a special way, a powerful attraction for the young is exercised by the commitment of priests to people hungry for God, for religious values and in a general condition of great spiritual poverty.[9]

It can also be seen that many young people discover the call to priesthood and to consecrated life after they have had an experience of doing *voluntary work*, in charitable service towards those who suffer, the needy and the poor, or after they have taken part for some time in Catholic missions.

Schools are another place in the life of boys and young men where, in meeting a priest who is a teacher or taking part in events to deepen their understanding of the Christian faith, they have begun a process of vocational discernment.

4. The spreading of a secularized mentality discourages the response of young people to follow the Lord Jesus more radically and more generously.

In response to the *Questionnaire* organized by the Pontifical Work for Priestly Vocations, the local Churches sent many replies that demonstrate a series of reasons why young men ignore a vocation to priestly ministry, putting it off to an unforeseeable future.

Parents, furthermore, with their hopes for their children's future, reserve little space to the possibility of a call to a special vocation.

Another aspect that goes against a priestly vocation is the gradual marginalization of the priest in social life, with the consequent loss of his relevance in the public sphere. Furthermore, in many places the choice of celibacy is questioned. Not only a secularized mentality, but also erroneous opinions within the Church bring about a lack of appreciation for the charism and the choice of celibacy. Furthermore, it is impossible to draw a veil of silence over the grave, negative effects of inconsistency and scandal caused by unfaithfulness to the duties of ministerial priesthood such as, for example, in the case of sexual abuse. This creates confusion in young men, even though they may otherwise be open to responding to the Lord's call.

The actual life of priests, drawn into the whirlpool of exaggerated activism with its consequent overload of pastoral work, can cloud and weaken the shine of priestly witness. In this situation, encouraging young men in their personal spiritual journeys and offering them spiritual accompaniment offer fruitful opportunities for suggesting or discerning a vocation, and especially a priestly vocation.

II

The Vocation and Identity of the Ministerial Priesthood

5. The identity of the vocation to the ministerial priesthood is to be understood within the context of Christian identity as a disciple of Christ. "The history of every priestly vocation, as indeed of every Christian vocation, is the history of an inexpressible dialogue between God and human beings, between the love of God who calls and the freedom of individuals who respond lovingly to him."[10]

The Gospels present vocation as a marvelous meeting between God and human beings. This is the mystery of being called, the mystery that involves the life of every Christian, but which is manifested with greater clarity in those whom Christ invites to leave everything to follow him more nearly. Christ has always chosen some persons to work together with him in a more direct manner for the realization of the Father's plan of salvation.

Before calling his disciples to a particular task, Jesus invites them to put everything to one side, to live in profound communion with him, indeed to "be" with him (Mk 3:14).[11]

Today, too, the Risen Lord calls future priests in order to transform them into true proclaimers of and witnesses to his saving presence in the world.

That experience is an example which shows the need to be travelling companions of the Risen Christ, setting out on a way of life that takes nothing for granted, but yields in openness to the Mystery of God who calls.

6. Christ the Shepherd is the origin and model of priestly ministry.[12] He himself has decided to entrust some of his disciples with the power to offer the Eucharistic sacrifice and to forgive sins.

"Thus Christ sent the apostles as he himself had been sent by the Father, and then through the apostles made their successors, the bishops, sharers in his consecration and mission. The function of the bishops' ministry was handed over in a subordinate degree to priests so that they might be appointed in the order of the priesthood and be co-workers of the episcopal order for the proper fulfillment of the apostolic mission that had been entrusted to it by Christ."[13]

For this reason, the priest, as well-attested by the doctrine of the *character* of Sacred Orders, is configured to Christ the Priest who enables him to act in the person of Christ the Head and Shepherd.[14] His being and his acting in ministry come from God's faithfulness, marked by the spiritual gift that, in the Sacrament of Orders, dwells in the priest in a permanent way and distinguishes him from the baptized who share in the common priesthood. The presbyter, in fact, inasmuch as he is united to the episcopal order, shares in the authority with which Christ "builds up and sanctifies and rules his Body."[15]

Ministerial priesthood is thus distinguished in essence from the common priesthood and is at its service.[16] Indeed, the ministerial priest "by the sacred power that he has, forms and rules the priestly people; in the person of Christ he effects the eucharistic sacrifice and offers it to God in the name of all the people. The faithful indeed, by virtue of their royal priesthood, participate in the offering of the Eucharist. They exercise that priesthood, too, by the reception of the sacraments, prayer and thanksgiving, the witness of a holy life, abnegation and active charity."[17] And "the ministry of priests is directed to this and finds its consummation in it."[18]

It is clear that the gift given by the laying on of hands has constantly to be "renewed" (see 2 Tm 1:6), so that "priests, whether they devote themselves to prayer and adoration, or preach the Word, or offer the eucharistic sacrifice and administer the other sacraments, or exercise other services for the benefit of men, are contributing at once to the increase of the glory of God and to men's growth in the divine life."[19] This first dimension of the Sacrament of Orders, its Christological character, forms the basis of its ecclesiological dimension.[20] Inasmuch as it is necessary that the Church herself is called together by the Risen Christ, priests are given the ability by the Sacrament of Orders to be effective instruments for the building up of the Church, by means of the proclamation of the Word, the celebration of the sacraments and guiding the People of God.[21] Without these gifts the Church would lose her identity. Ministerial priesthood is thus the vital and key point for the Church's existence, inasmuch as it is the effective sign of the priority of grace by which the Risen Christ builds up the Church in the Spirit.[22]

Therefore priests, representing Christ the Shepherd, find in their total dedication to the Church the unifying element of their theological identity and of their spiritual lives. For this reason "the primary point of reference of the priest's charity is Jesus Christ himself. Only in loving and serving Christ the head and spouse will charity become a source, criterion, measure and impetus for the priest's love and service to the Church, the body and spouse of Christ."[23] If ministerial priesthood does not find its origin in this love, it collapses into being the performance of a function, rather than the gift of the service of a shepherd who offers his life for the flock. It is, therefore, love for Christ that constitutes the overriding motivation for the vocation to the priesthood.

7. Priestly ministry, conferred by the Sacrament of Orders, in its nature is characterized by the life of the Trinity,[24] a life communicated by Christ and by his union with the Father in the Holy Spirit. This essentially describes priestly identity.[25]

The individual priest lives in a real and ontological communion with the presbyterate united to its bishop. Indeed: "By its very nature, the ordained ministry can be carried out only to the extent that the priest is united to Christ through sacramental participation in the priestly order, and thus to the extent that he is in hierarchical communion with his own bishop. The ordained ministry has a radical 'communitarian form' and can only be carried out as 'a collective work.'"[26]

The priest serves the *communio* of the Church in the name of Jesus Christ. The Lord calls the priest personally and brings him into a personal relationship with himself, with the experience of apostolic brotherhood and with the pastoral mission whose origin is supremely trinitarian. The apostolic "we," a reflection and a sharing in the communion of the Trinity, marks the identity of ordained ministry.[27]

It is clear that both the vocational journey and formation itself must engage with the essential elements of the trinitarian life,[28] characteristic of ordained ministry, where Christ's personal call is to serve a life of communion-mission reflecting the life of the Trinity.

An important task of vocational pastoral ministry, therefore, is that of offering boys and young men a Christian experience, by means of which they can know at first hand the reality of God Himself, in communion with their brothers and in Gospel mission.[29] Feeling part of a family of sons and daughters who have the same Father who loves them immensely, they are called to live as brothers and sisters and, persevering in unity, they place themselves at the service of the new evangelization "to proclaim and bear witness to the wonderful truth of the saving love of God."[30]

Pastoral ministry for vocations to ordained ministry is directed at generating men of communion and mission, capable of being inspired by the "new commandment" (Jn 13:34), the source of the "spirituality of communion."

The fostering of vocations and their consequent discernment greatly respect this Christian experience. It is the basis of a journey of grace written into the Sacrament of Orders and the condition for genuine evangelization.

8. A prudent and wise discernment of the essential conditions for being admitted to priesthood should be applied appropriately so as to be sure of the suitability of those who are "called." Pastoral ministry for vocations is aware that the response to the call is based upon the progressive integration of the personality's various components: human and Christian, personal and communitarian, cultural and pastoral.

Pastores Dabo Vobis says: "Knowledge of the nature and mission of the ministerial priesthood is an essential presupposition, and at the same time the surest guide and incentive toward the development of pastoral activities in the Church for fostering and discerning vocations to the priesthood and training those called to the ordained ministry."[31]

For this reason it is directed, in the first instance, to developing the whole person and, in the context of a profound communitarian experience, aims at preparing those "called" for priesthood, helping them be conformed to Christ the Shepherd.

Whoever is called should be placed in the condition of living an intimate relationship of love with the Father who calls him, with the Son who conforms him, with the Spirit who shapes him through training in prayer, listening to the Word, participation in the Eucharist and silent adoration.

Growing in vocation develops hand in hand with gradually taking on tasks, choices, responsibilities. This also allows a deep and wide-ranging discernment of the authenticity of a person's vocation.

The integration and maturing of the affections are necessary for knowing how to welcome the grace of the Sacrament. Proposing a vocation should be avoided to persons who, even though they are praiseworthy in their journey of conversion, show signs of being profoundly fragile personalities.

It is important that whoever is called should see with clarity the commitments he will have to take on, in particular with regard to celibacy.[32]

It is helpful that anyone called should be rooted in a precise ecclesial context, which supports the reasons for his choice of vocation and contributes to healing any possible individual deviations from his vocation.[33] In this way, the quality of his parochial and diocesan experience, as well as his participation in Church activities, associations, and movements, acquires a fundamental importance.[34]

It would normally be good for boys and young men to have an experience of community life before going to seminary.

9. A decisive role is played by vocation directors, who often take the place of the priest who nourished and sustained the beginnings of a vocation. Both the educational relationship with facilitators and the quality of brotherhood with others who have been called, make the discernment of a vocational choice more authentic and valid.

Without doubt, since priests' public profiles can give an idea of the figure of a priest and the conditions of his ministry in ordinary life, the life of individual priests and of the entire diocesan presbyterate can favor the development of a priestly call.

The figures of priests venerated as saints contribute in no small way to the courage and generosity of those who are called. Priests completely dedicated to their pastoral ministry are secure models and reference points for consolidating a man's motives for choosing priestly ordination.

It is sufficient to remember St. John Mary Vianney, the Holy Curé d'Ars, who, during the 2010 Year for Priests, was indicated by the Holy

Father Benedict XVI as a shining model for all priests. Along with him, we could remember many other exemplary priests who, with self-denial over the ages, have accompanied the progress of the People of God in the various local Churches.

Certainly, it is important to call trustingly and persistently upon the Virgin Mary, Mother of Priests, for help in welcoming with openness God's plan for our lives. We ask her help to respond "yes," with faith and love, to the Lord who always calls new laborers to spread the Kingdom of God.

10. The growth and nurture of a priestly vocation demands love in service for one's own particular Church, as well as complete availability to undertake any kind of pastoral service. An experience of inner freedom will come from not feeling as if one owns one's vocation.

Active participation in the life of a Christian community can contribute to avoiding new forms of clericalism, situations of inopportune pastoral centralism, merely part-time pastoral services, ministerial choices that revolve around one's own individual needs and the inability to see the bigger picture and the unity of the community.

To build a Church into a state of permanent mission, the vocation of the priest is lived in such a way as to develop a community rich in ministries, where there is ample space for the active participation and responsibility of the lay faithful.

So as to be able to lead and sustain a community, it is useful for young men called to the priesthood to learn to work together and dialogue with the whole Christian community and to value every vocation.

The universal dimension is intrinsic to priestly ministry.[35] Ordination makes the priest fit for mission, which is an essential aspect of priestly identity.

In this sense, it is important to educate whoever is called to be concerned for his neighbors and, at the same time, to look to those who are far off.

Availability for mission defines the truth of the priest in each of his activities. This means developing an inner structure and a way of being, more than a way of doing, that is distinguished by its courage in going beyond any kind of particularity in order to open one's heart to the needs of the new evangelization.

III

Suggestions for Pastoral Ministry for Priestly Vocations

11. Priestly vocations are the fruit of the Holy Spirit's action in the Church. In some countries there is a vigorous and promising flowering of priestly vocations, which is an encouragement to continue fostering vocations.

The Church, aware of the need for vocations to the priesthood, recognizes that they are a gift from God and prays to the Lord with incessant and trusting supplication that he will be generous in giving them.

"It is really God himself, the 'Lord of the harvest,' who chooses his laborers; his call is always undeserved and unexpected. And yet, in the mystery of God's covenant with us, we are called to cooperate with his providence, and to use the powerful tool which he has placed in our hands: prayer! This is what Jesus himself asked us to do: 'Pray the Lord of the harvest to send out laborers into his harvest!'"[36]

Prayer moves the heart of God. For believers, prayer becomes the great school of life, teaching them to look with evangelical wisdom at the world and at the needs of each human being. Above all, it unites hearts to the same charity and compassion of Christ for humanity.[37]

The experience of many local Churches is that young men, in large numbers, sense the call to ministerial priesthood, especially where prayer is a constant and profound dimension of the community's life.

12. In the West, there is a prevailing culture of indifference to the Christian faith, a culture unable to understand the value of vocations to a special consecration.

Nonetheless, the Church, which is called to live in the present, looks with wisdom to history where she sees the presence of God who accompanies, challenges, calls people into covenant with him even in the moments that are apparently the least fertile and fruitful. She looks "with immense sympathy upon the world because, even if the world feels itself estranged from Christianity, the Church cannot feel itself estranged from the world, whatever the attitude of the world may be towards the Church."[38]

Still today, the Church continues to proclaim the Word of God and to communicate the Good News of salvation with the courage that comes from the truth. In particular, she tries to set before boys and young men the life-challenging faith that responds to the thirst for happiness residing in the human heart.

This means offering the experience of faith as a personal, profound relationship with the Lord Jesus Christ, the One who reveals the Mystery of God.

The discovery of a vocation is born from a response of faith, especially when it is lived within Christian communities where the beauty of the Gospel is lived and where leaders and educators are capable of perceiving the signs of a vocation.

In order to make real what the Christian faith proposes, which then leads to a response in terms of a vocation, genuine human relationships[39] need to be encouraged. This should be done by educators and adult mentors in the faith, in the context of communities that have an attractive and exciting Christian life.

It is advisable to be open in offering the possibility of priestly life to boys and young men and, at the same time, it is necessary to invite Christian communities to pray more intensely to "the Lord of the harvest" (Mt 9:38) that he may raise up new ministers and new consecrated people.

To do this, it is useful to support a general pastoral ministry in the local Churches, which is characterized by evangelical, vocational, and missionary enthusiasm.

13. All the members of the Church are responsible for looking after priestly vocations. "The Second Vatican Council was quite explicit in this regard: 'The duty of fostering vocations falls on the whole Christian community, and they should discharge it principally by living full Christian lives' [*Optatam Totius*, no. 2]. Only on the basis of this conviction will pastoral work on behalf of vocations be able to show its truly ecclesial aspect,

develop a harmonious plan of action, and make use of specific agencies and appropriate instruments of communion and co-responsibility."[40]

Already seventy years ago, the Holy See instituted the *Pontifical Work for Priestly Vocations* with the aim of supporting collaboration between the Holy See and the local Churches in promoting vocations to ordained ministry.

This office has worked to spread awareness of the *Message for the World Day of Prayer for Vocations* which the Holy Father addresses every year to the whole Church. Furthermore, it has the task of gathering and disseminating news of the most significant initiatives with regard to vocations undertaken by the local Churches. It also organizes international Conferences; and it promotes and collaborates in organizing the Continental Conferences, with the aim of helping to produce a synergy among those active in the field of pastoral ministry for vocations.

The experience of the past few decades shows that the Holy Father's Message helps local Churches to construct, recommend and realize annual programs of pastoral ministry for vocations.

The bishop's role in promoting vocations, and in particular priestly vocations, is central and pre-eminent. "The first responsibility for the pastoral work of promoting priestly vocations lies with the bishop [*Christus Dominus*, no. 15], who is called to be the first to exercise this responsibility even though he can and must call upon many others to cooperate with him. As the father and friend of his presbyterate, it falls primarily to the bishop to be concerned about 'giving continuity' to the priestly charism and ministry, bringing it new forces by the laying on of hands. He will be actively concerned to ensure that the vocational dimension is always present in the whole range of ordinary pastoral work, and that it is fully integrated and practically identified with it. It is his duty to foster and coordinate various initiatives on behalf of vocations."[41]

The bishop has the task of ensuring that youth pastoral ministry and vocations pastoral ministry are entrusted to priests and others who are capable of transmitting, with enthusiasm and with the example of their lives, the joy of following the Lord Jesus in the school of the Gospel.

At a diocesan level, the bishop is the one who establishes the Diocesan Office for Vocations, made up of priests, consecrated persons and lay people. This instrument of communion serves pastoral ministry for vocations in the local Church, and has the task of fostering vocations of special consecration within the context of all vocations.

The Office for Vocations looks after the formation of vocations advisers, advances and spreads a vocational culture within the People of God, shares in the planning of the diocesan pastoral program, and in particular works together with the diocesan offices for family pastoral ministry, catechesis and youth pastoral ministry.

Vocational groups that offer a program of Christian education and a first chance to test vocations are to be encouraged and supported in dioceses and in parishes.[42]

National or interdiocesan vocational offices, commissioned by the Bishops' Conferences and, normally, under the guidance of a bishop, coordinate the Diocesan Offices for Vocations.

14. The grace of the call finds fertile ground in a Church that, through its communities and all the faithful, creates the conditions for free and generous vocational responses.

Blessed John Paul II asked the bishops "to reinvigorate the social fabric of the Christian community by means of the evangelization of the family; assist the laity to enliven the values of consistency, justice, and Christian charity in the world of youth."[43]

In our times, the witness of Christian communities giving account of the faith that is in them becomes even more necessary, so that Christians, committed to following Christ, can pass on his love. The communion of believers in Christ prepares the Lord's call that invites people to consecration and mission.

The fostering of the priestly vocation first takes place in Christian families. If they are animated by a spirit of faith, charity and piety they become, as it were, an "initial seminary" (see *Optatam Totius*, no. 2) and they continue "to offer favorable conditions for the birth of vocations."[44]

Even though a sense of respect for the figure of the priest is cultivated in Christian families, it is still noticeable, especially in the West, that they have a certain difficulty in accepting that their child may have a vocation to the priesthood or to a special consecration.

An educational overlap exists between family and vocational pastoral ministries. Thus, it is necessary to make parents more aware of their ministry, rooted in the Sacrament of Marriage, as educators in the faith, so as to develop in the heart of the family the human and supernatural conditions that make possible the discovery of a priestly vocation.

For its part, the parish is the place *par excellence* where the Gospel of the Christian vocation is proclaimed and, in particular, where the ideal of priestly ministry is presented. It is the fertile ground where vocations develop and mature, on the condition that it gather together "the family of God as a brotherhood fired with a single ideal, and through Christ in the Spirit . . . lead him to God the Father"[45] and, therefore, it should be characterized by a way of living like that of the first Christians (see Acts 2:42; 4:32).

The variety of vocations is obvious in the parish, and the urgent need for priests to celebrate the Eucharist and the Sacrament of Reconciliation is clear and pressing.

The parish community is a fruitful womb, capable of offering a valuable contribution of human and spiritual formation to those who journey towards priestly ministry.

Priests and consecrated people, above all those who work in the parish communities, are crucial for openly suggesting priestly vocation to boys and young men, with the aid of a well-founded and effective educational programme that is capable of bringing the question of vocation to the fore.

Catechists and the organizers of parish pastoral work, too, while they teach the whole of the Christian message, can identify and offer valuable links between catechetical themes and the presentation of specific vocations, especially the vocation to the priesthood. "Particularly catechists, teachers, educators and youth ministers, each with his or her own resources and style, have great importance in the pastoral work of promoting priestly vocations: The more they inculcate a deep appreciation of young people's vocation and mission in the Church, the more they will be able to recognize the unique value of the priestly vocation and mission."[46]

15. Seminarians should be reminded of an established pastoral truth: "No one is better suited to evangelize young people than young people themselves. Young students who are preparing for the presbyterate, young men and women who are undergoing formation as religious or as missionaries, personally and as communities are the first and most immediate apostles of vocation in the midst of other young people."[47] Furthermore, organized ecclesial groups, movements and associations are to be born in mind, in that they are valuable educational places for openness to a priestly vocation. Within them, the encounter with Christ is favoured by attention to individuals, offering clear spiritual content and being rooted in prayer. More than a few vocations have been born from these experiences.[48]

Teachers in schools are committed to a service that, by its nature, is a vocation and mission. They can extent the family's educational role by broadening cultural horizons and ought never to forget life's vocational dimension.

Their service can open young people to a life-choice of total self-gift to God and to other people, infusing "in the hearts of boys and young men a desire to do God's will in that state in life which is most suitable to each person, and never excluding the vocation to the priestly ministry."[49]

Time at university is also, in many countries, becoming a fruitful period for young people with regard to their life-choices. This deserves the closest attention: the years of youth are precious and decisive in the search for the full meaning of one's existence.

Those who organize leisure pursuits and sport in church institutions, over and above the specific reasons inspiring these activities and the human values they allow to be realized, must not forget their higher aim: the holistic and harmonious formation of the person. This kind of human formation, in the measure it agrees with the principles of Christian education, is in reality fertile ground for proposing a priestly vocation.

Spiritual direction is a privileged form of discernment and of vocational accompaniment. What is asked of priests is a sincere openness to listening and dialogue, the capacity to raise and reply to the fundamental questions of existence, a great deal of wisdom in dealing with the questions inherent in life-choices and in the vocation to priestly ministry.

Spiritual direction and vocational counselling demand a specific preparation in the initial and ongoing formation of priests.

16. The key things to foster priestly vocations are those proposed by formation for Christian life: listening to the Word of God, participation in the Eucharist and exercising charity.

The proclamation of the Word passes through preaching and establishes and underscores the ways and forms of putting the Gospel into practice in the life of individuals and of ecclesial communities: "We need a 'direct preaching on the mystery of vocation in the Church, on the value of the ministerial priesthood, on God's people.'"[50]

Catechesis is also an ordinary way for fostering vocations when it helps children and young people to give value to life as a response to God, and when it supports them in accepting in faith the gift of a personal vocation.

Catechesis in preparation for the Sacrament of Confirmation is a chance to let those who are being confirmed know the gifts of the Spirit, the charisms, the ministries and the various callings linked to them.

No kind of catechesis should overlook the presentation of the priestly vocation: "A properly structured catechesis, directed to all the members of the Church, in addition to dissipating doubts and countering one-sided or distorted ideas about priestly ministry, will open believers' hearts to expect the gift and create favorable conditions for the birth of new vocations."[51]

The Eucharist, center of Christian life and of the community, allows one to set out a sacramental and liturgical path that is capable of nourishing regularly the progress of every vocation.

Going frequently and regularly to the Sacrament of Reconciliation also is decisive in discerning a priestly vocation.

The liturgical year is the Christian community's permanent school of faith. It punctuates the times and moments of everyday life and supports the ripening of vocations among the faithful.

Prayer initiatives, and most especially Eucharistic adoration, which are prepared and conducted in a meaningful way and with a profound liturgical sense, can highlight the extraordinary importance of the priestly vocation.

The witness of charity finds a multiform and surprising expression in the Church. It is vital that these kinds of initiatives should be reinforced by means of precise programs of formation that stimulate generosity and service to the Kingdom of God and that configure individuals and communities to Christ.

The sensitivity of young people to the conditions of the weak and the poor is growing. Many show themselves ready to serve, to identify themselves with their neighbor's joys and difficulties in life.

Some choose charitable voluntary work as a way of serving those who suffer, the elderly and the poor. Others are committed to educating children: by teaching catechism, in Catholic associations, or in free-time activities. There are also those who give a valuable witness in volunteering for missionary work with its powerful capacity to change a person's life, opening him or her to the pressing and serious material and spiritual needs widespread in developing countries.

Vocations that grow up in an environment of a Christian witness of charity are solid and genuine, motivated in earnest by service.

17. In ecclesial communities it is necessary to encourage a true and real movement of prayer to ask the Lord for vocations. In fact, "Christian prayer, nourished by the word of God, creates an ideal environment where each individual can discover the truth of his own being and the identity of the personal and unrepeatable life project which the Father entrusts to him. It is therefore necessary to educate boys and young men so that they will become faithful to prayer and meditation on God's word: in silence and listening, they will be able to perceive the Lord who is calling them to the priesthood, and be able to follow that call promptly and generously."[52]

Initiatives that display a harmonious community in prayer for vocations should be supported and increased.

Thus it would be good for the Diocesan Office for Vocations to propose and organize an "invisible monastery" in which many persons, day and night, are committed to continuous prayer for priestly vocations.

"Vocations Thursday" is a traditional moment of monthly communal prayer, centered around Eucharistic adoration, for priests and priestly vocations.

The "World Day of Prayer for Vocations" and "Seminary Day" are two noteworthy moments for prayer, catechesis, and proclaiming the possibility of vocations to the Christian community.

18. Altar service is often the first step to other forms of service in the Christian community. This experience, wisely integrated into education for liturgical prayer, listening to the Word and sacramental life, can be used as a real path leading to the possibility of a priestly vocation.

For this reason, vocational ministry for priesthood gives special attention to altar boys. Numerous priests and seminarians, before going to seminary, have been part of the group of altar boys and have served at the altar.

Retreats and vocational spiritual exercises, organized for young men, are extremely important in allowing them to live the experience of silence, of prolonged prayer and of encountering the Word of God. They can be special moments of reflection upon one's life, a personal discovery of one's own vocation.

"Residential vocational communities" can also help young men in finding and discerning a vocational direction leading to the seminary. They are a kind of "pre-seminary," with the stable presence of properly trained priests who offer a "rule of life" punctuated by moments of brotherly life, personal study, sharing in the Word, personal and communal prayer, celebrating the Eucharist and spiritual direction.

19. Minor seminaries can offer boys and teenagers the chance to be accompanied, educated, and formed in discerning their desire to become priests. Furthermore: "In view of its nature and mission, the minor seminary could well become a significant reference point for vocations promotion in the diocese, with suitable formative experiences for young men seeking to discover the direction of their lives and their vocation, and for those who have already decided to set out on the path to ministerial priesthood, but are not yet ready to enter the major seminary."[53]

Conclusion

20. Fostering vocations to the priesthood is a constant challenge for the Church.

On the occasion of the seventieth anniversary of its inauguration, the Pontifical Work for Priestly Vocations, in order to encourage all Christian communities and those in them especially involved in pastoral ministry for vocations, offers this document to the particular Churches as a compendium on fostering vocations to the ministerial priesthood.

The most favorable environment for vocations to the priesthood is every Christian community that listens to the Word of God, prays with the liturgy and gives witness with charity. In this context, the mission of a priest is most clearly perceived and recognized.

This document wishes to support ecclesial communities, associations, and movements in their commitment to fostering vocations, directing their efforts towards a pastoral ministry for vocations capable of nurturing every life-choice of self-giving and which fosters, in particular, a welcome for the call of God to ministerial priesthood.

The Holy Father approved the present document and authorized its publication.

Rome, March 25, 2012, Solemnity of the Annunciation of the Lord.

Zenon Cardinal Grocholewski
Prefect

+Jean-Louis Bruguès
Secretary

Notes

1. The Plenary Assembly of the Congregation for Catholic Education dealt with this theme in its meetings of 2005 and 2008.

2. "Especially in some regions, indeed precisely the very small number of young priests represents already now a serious problem for pastoral work. Together with the whole Christian community, we trustingly ask and humbly beg the Lord for the gift of new and holy workers for his harvest (cf. Mt 9:37-38). We know that the Lord sometimes makes us wait, but we also know that no one knocks in vain. So, with patient confidence we continue to pray to the Lord for the gift of new holy 'laborers'" (Benedict XVI, Address to the Members of the Italian Episcopal Conference Gathered for their 57th General Assembly, May 24, 2007).

3. Benedict XVI, Homily for the Mass with the Members of the Bishops' Conference of Switzerland (November 7, 2006).

4. "Let us surround these brothers of ours in the Lord with our spiritual solidarity. Let us pray that they may be faithful to the mission to which the Lord is calling them today and ready to renew their 'yes' to God, their 'here I am,' every day without reserve" (Pope Benedict XVI, Homily at Mass for the ordination of priests of the diocese of Rome, April 29, 2007).

5. Pope John Paul II, Post-Synodal Apostolic Exhortation *Pastores Dabo Vobis* (*I Will Give You Shepherds*), March 25, 1992, no. 41.

6. See *Pastores Dabo Vobis*, no. 68.

7. *Pastores Dabo Vobis*, no. 41.

8. "The service of love is the fundamental meaning of every vocation, and it finds a specific expression in the priestly vocation" (*Pastores Dabo Vobis*, no. 40).

9. "Your enthusiasm, your communion and your life of prayer and generous ministry are indispensable. It can happen that you feel weariness or fear as you face the new demands and problems, but we must trust that the Lord will give us the necessary strength to do what he asks of us. He—let us pray and we are sure—will never let vocations be lacking if we implore him with prayer and at the same time are concerned to seek and foster them with a fervent and imaginative youth and vocations ministry, which can reveal the beauty of the priestly ministry" (Pope Benedict XVI, Address at Meeting in Assisi with Clergy and Men and Women Religious in the Cathedral of Saint Rufinus, June 17, 2007).

10. *Pastores Dabo Vobis*, no. 36.

11. See *Pastores Dabo Vobis*, no. 34.

12. See *Pastores Dabo Vobis*, no. 23.

13. Second Vatican Council, Decree on the Ministry and Life of Priests *Presbyterorum Ordinis*, no. 2, in *Vatican Council II: Volume 1: The Conciliar and Post Conciliar Documents*, ed. Austin Flannery (Northport, NY: Costello Publishing, 1996); see Second Vatican Council, Dogmatic Constitution on the Church *Lumen Gentium*, no. 28, in *Vatican Council II: Volume 1: The Conciliar and Post Conciliar Documents*, ed. Austin Flannery (Northport, NY: Costello Publishing, 1996).

14. See *Presbyterorum Ordinis*, no. 2.

15. *Presbyterorum Ordinis*, no. 2.

16. See *Lumen Gentium*, no. 10.

17. *Lumen Gentium*, no. 10.

18. *Presbyterorum Ordinis*, no. 2.

19. *Presbyterorum Ordinis*, no. 2.

20. See, no. 16.

21. See *Presbyterorum Ordinis*, nos. 4-6.

22.   See *Pastores Dabo Vobis*, no. 15.

23.   *Pastores Dabo Vobis*, no. 23.

24.   "'The priest's identity,' as the synod fathers wrote, 'like every Christian identity, has its source in the Blessed Trinity.' . . . It is within the Church's mystery, as a mystery of Trinitarian communion in missionary tension, that every Christian identity is revealed, and likewise the specific identity of the priest and his ministry. Indeed, the priest, by virtue of the consecration which he receives in the sacrament of orders, is sent forth by the Father through the mediatorship of Jesus Christ, to whom he is configured in a special way as head and shepherd of his people, in order to live and work by the power of the Holy Spirit in service of the Church and for the salvation of the world" (*Pastores Dabo Vobis*, no. 12).

25.   "In this way the fundamentally 'relational' dimension of priestly identity can be understood. Through the priesthood which arises from the depths of the ineffable mystery of God, that is, from the love of the Father, the grace of Jesus Christ and the Holy Spirit's gift of unity, the priest sacramentally enters into communion with the bishop and with other priests in order to serve the People of God who are the Church and to draw all mankind to Christ" (*Pastores Dabo Vobis*, no. 12).

26.   *Pastores Dabo Vobis*, no. 17.

27.   See *Presbyterorum Ordinis*, nos. 7-9.

28.   See *Pastores Dabo Vobis*, no. 17.

29.   "Before making practical plans, we need to promote a spirituality of communion, making it the guiding principle of education wherever individuals and Christians are formed, wherever ministers of the altar, consecrated persons, and pastoral workers are trained, wherever families and communities are being built up" (Pope John Paul II, Apostolic Letter *Novo Millennio Ineunte*, January 6, 2001, no. 43).

30.   Pope John Paul II, Message for the 42nd World Day of Prayer for Vocations (April 17, 2005).

31.   *Pastores Dabo Vobis*, no. 11.

32.   "The formation for celibacy of candidates for the priesthood deserves particular mention. It is important that they learn to live and to esteem celibacy as a precious gift from God and as an eminently eschatological sign which bears witness to an undivided love for God and for his people, and configures the priest to Jesus Christ, Head and Bridegroom of the Church. This gift, in fact, in an outstanding way 'expresses the priest's service to the Church in and with the Lord' and has a prophetic value for today's world" (Pope Benedict XVI, Letter to the Bishops, Priests, Consecrated Persons and Lay Faithful of the Catholic Church in the People's Republic of China (May 27, 2007), no. 14).

33.   See *Pastores Dabo Vobis*, no. 9.

34.   See *Pastores Dabo Vobis*, no. 68.

35.   See Congregation for the Clergy, *Directory for the Ministry and Life of Priests*, nos. 14-15.

36.   Pope John Paul II, Speech to the Members of Serra International (December 7, 2000); cf. Speech to the Serra International Movement (March 29, 1980), original text in *Insegnamenti* 111-1 (1980), 759-761.

37.   See Pope John Paul II, Message for the 38th World Day of Prayer for Vocations (May 6, 2001).

38.   Pope Paul VI, Speech on the Solemnity of the Epiphany at the Holy Grotto of Bethlehem (January 6, 1964): AAS 56 (1964), 177; *L'Osservatore Romano* Anno CIV, no. 5 (January 7-8, 1964), 2.

39.   See *Novo Millennio Ineunte*, no. 45.

40.   *Pastores Dabo Vobis*, no. 41.

41.   *Pastores Dabo Vobis*, no. 41; see Second Vatican Council, Decree on Priestly Formation *Optatam Totius*, no. 2, in *Vatican Council II: Volume 1: The Conciliar and Post Conciliar Documents*, ed. Austin Flannery (Northport, NY: Costello Publishing, 1996); see also *Code of Canon Law* (*Codex Iuris Canonici* [CIC]) (Washington, DC: Canon Law Society of America, 1998), c. 385.

42.   See *Pastores Dabo Vobis*, no. 41.

43.   Pope John Paul II, Message for the 30th World Day of Prayer for Vocations (May 2, 1993).

44.   *Pastores Dabo Vobis*, no. 41.

45.   *Lumen Gentium*, no. 28.

46.   *Pastores Dabo Vobis*, no. 41.

47.   Congregations for the Oriental Churches, for Religious and Secular Institutes, for the Evangelization of Peoples, for Catholic Education (eds.), *Developments in the Pastoral Care for Vocations in the Particular Churches: Past Experiences and Plans for the Future* (final document of the Second International Congress of Bishops and Others Responsible for Ecclesiastical Vocations, Rome, May 10-16, 1981) (May 2, 1982), no. 41.

48.   See *Pastores Dabo Vobis*, no. 41.

49.   *Pastores Dabo Vobis*, no. 41; see Congregation for Catholic Education, *Educating Together in Catholic Schools* (September 8, 2007), no. 19.

50.   *Pastores Dabo Vobis*, no. 39.

51.   *Pastores Dabo Vobis*, no. 39.

52.   *Pastores Dabo Vobis*, no. 38.

53.   Congregation for Bishops, Directory for the Pastoral Ministry of Bishops *Apostolorum Successores* (February 22, 2004), no. 86.